Wonderfully Made is the perfect companion for any pregnancy. Whether you're a first-time mom or a mom to many, taking time each week to recognize God's presence along your journey and to document your experience will be a gift not only to yourself but also to the precious child growing within you. Wonderful!

LISA M. HENDEY, *founder of CatholicMom.com and author of The Handbook for Catholic Moms*

Wonderfully Made is a beautiful companion for the journey of pregnancy. Each entry offers grounding wisdom in the form of suggested Scripture, a prayerful reflection, practical advice, and even a space to write down responses and prayers. The book is a great resource to help a mom-to-be to stay anchored in her prayer during the awe-inspiring (and often disorienting) months of pregnancy.

NICHOLE M. FLORES, *Assistant Professor of Religious Studies at University of Virginia and contributing author at America magazine*

This simple journal is a beautiful way to commemorate those special weeks of anticipating the arrival of a new baby to love. Clarissa Aljentera walks us through many of the emotions and experiences of pregnancy while incorporating elements of faith. A creative and thoughtful gift for any expectant mother!

DANIELLE BEAN, *Brand Manager, CatholicMom.com*

My own experience of pregnancy was long ago now, and I regret that I suffer from the "Momnesia" Aljentera talks about. I wish that I'd had a resource like this to record reflections along the way so that I'd be able to continue to savor insights from that most special time in life and to share them with my son as he stands on the edge of embracing marriage and family life. Truly, the marvel of pregnancy is something that we will want, like Mary, to continue to ponder long after our child has been born.

ANN GARRIDO, *Associate Professor of Homiletics, Aquinas Institute of Theology*

Wonderfully Made

A WEEKLY JOURNAL

for FAITH-FILLED

MOMS-TO-BE

CLARISSA VALBUENA ALJENTERA

**TWENTY-THIRD
PUBLICATIONS**
twentythirdpublications.com

Dedication

To Alfred

You inspire me to do great things.

I'm forever lucky you took a chance on a wink.

To AJ

You made me a mama.

I can't wait to see the plans God has for you.

TWENTY-THIRD PUBLICATIONS
One Montauk Avenue, Suite 200 • New London, CT 06320
(860) 437-3012 or (800) 321-0411 • www.twentythirdpublications.com

Cover art: ©iStockphoto.com / goodgraphic

ISBN: 978-1-62785-468-9 • Printed in the U.S.A.

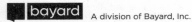 A division of Bayard, Inc.

CONTENTS

Introduction

Congratulations! No matter where you are in the pregnancy journey, know that God is walking with you through it all. This time of anticipation and joy will be both beautiful and challenging.

Wherever you are in your faith journey, know that this journal is meant to help you capture the beauty of growing another human inside you and the life that comes along with this vocation of motherhood. Open yourself to the transformation from wife to mother. Take time to breathe into this new life. Pregnancy will stretch you physically and emotionally as you prepare to make room in your heart and your life for your baby.

This journal was written to help you enter spiritually into your pregnancy in a simple and engaging way. Maybe you're an early riser and love journaling first thing with a cup of tea. Or your lifestyle might be such that throwing some thoughts on paper at the end of the day is much more your speed. Maybe you are hopeful that this pregnancy is another way to deepen your faith and to put your trust in God's hands. Or maybe you are thinking about how many prayers and novenas were shared to help you conceive, and you want to keep praying until your baby is born. Whatever you come seeking for yourself, know that it can be found through your own prayer and maybe even in these words you write down on these pages.

Blessings on this beautiful journey of life! And happy writing!

A Beautiful Secret

My very self you know.
My bones are not
hidden from you, when
I was being made in
secret, fashioned in the
depths of the earth.
Your eyes saw me
unformed; in your book
all are written down;
my days were shaped,
before one came to be.

PSALM 139:14–16

*Y*ou are growing a human person inside you. You likely don't know even it—but something beautiful is taking place. Science describes it as cells dividing rapidly to create your baby's organs, their cute features, and their living being. God describes it as creation—an opportunity for you and your husband's love to flourish.

There is a beautiful secret deep inside of you that will change your life forever—whether you are ready or not. Psalm 139 describes the secrets that only God knows. We learn of all the amazing things that God knows about your life and your baby's life too: "My very self you know. My bones are not hidden from you, when I was being made in secret, fashioned as in the depths of the earth. Your eyes saw me unformed; in your book all are written down; my days were shaped, before one came to be."

 What does it feel like to know of these secrets God has growing inside of you? How do feel about placing your trust in God's hands?

_____

_____

_____

_____

_____

_____

_____

_____

_____

Anxiety and Worry

"Can any of you by worrying add a single moment to your life-span?"

MATTHEW 6:27

In a few short weeks you may have to answer the question "Were you trying or is this a surprise?" Even if the pregnancy is a total shock, God knew this was planned. It was somehow planned in the busyness of your life as you were balancing home and work. Maybe it was planned when it was just bad timing to have a child. Or maybe the baby is the intention you brought to Mass every Sunday in the quiet of your heart.

God knows what's in your heart long before you ever do. In this time of transition do not be afraid to give all your desires, fears, and anxieties to God. As Jesus tells us: "Can any of you by worrying add a single moment to your life-span?"

What makes you anxious about the baby?
What frightens you about moving forward?
Is there peace in knowing a baby is on the way?

_____

_____

_____

_____

_____

_____

_____

_____

Making Room for Joy

She is clothed with strength and dignity and laughs at the days to come.

PROVERBS 31:25

Maybe you notice something different about your body. Or maybe you don't notice anything yet.

The next eight months will feel like a marathon as your body changes and your mind begins to shift. A new strength will be required, and you will find it. In the Book of Proverbs, we see a strong image of a mother who can handle all that her household asks of her: "She is clothed with strength and dignity and laughs at the days to come." This image helps us see that there is joy in the future, even with all that lies ahead.

When you were growing up, where did you see your mom encounter joy? How are you hoping to find joy as a mother? Where do you see your strength growing as you prepare for your baby?

God's Creation

God created mankind in his image; in the image of God he created them; male and female he created them.

GENESIS 1:27

This week you may just be learning that you and your husband are expecting, and perhaps you are wondering if it's too early to tell family and close friends. Some couples wait until twelve weeks to share the news, and others let people know much earlier. The choice is yours and your husband's. There is no right or wrong way. It depends on your personal comfort; and when you are ready, you are ready. Some couples opt for a fun reveal complete with homemade videos, signs, or FaceTime conversations.

This time of knowing that you and your husband are pregnant is precious and special to the two of you. This baby growing inside you is the child that makes you parents. Cherish these moments before releasing your secret to the world. It's exciting to think about how this news is shared. There is much joy and elation in knowing a human is growing inside you. In Genesis we see

God creating something large and small: "God created mankind in his image; in the image of God he created them; male and female he created them." Your own creation story is reflected in this.

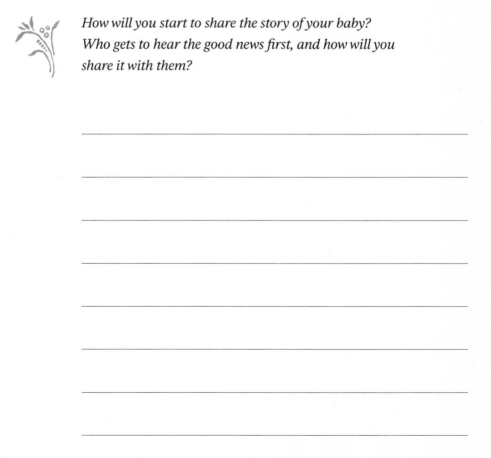

How will you start to share the story of your baby?
Who gets to hear the good news first, and how will you
share it with them?

_____

_____

_____

_____

_____

_____

_____

Good News

"Hail, favored one!
The Lord is with you."

LUKE 1:28

erhaps it was the home pregnancy test that confirmed your good news. An inner hunch led you to make a quick trip to the drug store or grab a pregnancy test from your bathroom. Perhaps those indicator lines that showed pregnancy were a surprise. Maybe your mind began racing, or tears fell.

You could jump up and down and hug everyone you encounter the rest of the day. Your joy is contagious, and you hope and pray this pregnancy is the real deal. Whatever the journey looks like the next eight months, your baby is special and unique from its very beginning. This time of preparation and growing into motherhood holds much promise and wonder for you. Let yourself rest in the affirmation of motherhood. In the Gospel of Luke, we see Mary being visited by the angel Gabriel with these words: "Hail, favored one! The Lord is with you."

 Imagine it's you in that gospel passage being celebrated with the news of your child. What do you think about your own Good News being shared with you today? What will you share with God about this moment of joy? If the angel had appeared to you, what would you say?

_____

_____

_____

_____

_____

_____

_____

_____

_____

A Unique Name

*Of her was born
Jesus who is called
the Messiah.*

MATTHEW 1:16

There are so many discussions you and your husband will be having in the coming weeks. You will have to decide which optional blood tests you will take, if you are of a certain age. You may also decide on genetic testing, if that's an option. You will start compiling baby names and possibly decide if you want to find out your child's gender. Somehow, God has already decided that the baby growing inside you belongs to you. The features and traits have already been decided.

It's magical and maybe paralyzing when you stop to think about how many things you want to know the answer to as a first-time mom. Take heart and take pause in all that will unfold. In all this excitement you are thinking about names for boys and girls—even if you are keeping it to yourself at this point. Maybe you are researching names or looking at family names to pass down. There's a reason you were given your

name, and a good reason your baby will have his or her name. In the Gospel of Matthew in the first chapter we see a long list of names that point to the genealogy of Jesus including the title *Messiah*.

As your baby name lists are starting, what does it mean to you to give your child their unique name? What are some of the names you are thinking about? Why are these names important to you and your husband?

Wisdom and Knowledge

Wisdom builds her house, but Folly tears hers down with her own hands.

PROVERBS 14:1

The information available to moms today can be overwhelming. Perhaps you will be seeking an obstetrician and the right books to read during your pregnancy. You may find yourself downloading apps onto your phone that show the baby's progress.

Information and knowledge about your pregnancy can be a real gift. It is comforting to know if your baby is the size of a blueberry, a grape, or a raspberry this week. Following your pregnancy journey closely on the outside helps you connect with your baby on the inside. As you follow your baby's development, you may feel with each passing week that your heart grows a little more, knowing that you and your baby are getting ready for the debut to the outside world. In the Book of Proverbs we see Wisdom building her house. "Wisdom builds her house, but Folly tears hers down with her own hands."

 What are some of your favorite websites, books, or apps for learning more about pregnancy? Why did you choose them? What's one thing you have learned about your baby recently that has surprised you?

_____

_____

_____

_____

_____

_____

_____

_____

Trusting in God

I have stilled my soul,
like a weaned child
to its mother, weaned
is my soul.

PSALM 131:2

You may not see it yet, but things are changing rapidly. Slowly your body is nurturing your baby. Emotionally and physically, the changes are real. There is a beautiful transformation on the horizon. You will move from being a wife to wife *and* mother. Somehow there will be more room in your home and your heart for your beloved.

Take stock of your body now before it morphs into something even more beautiful. Somehow there will be time and space to nurture all that is growing. Trust in God to guide you through this journey. Becoming a mother builds on a lifetime of experiences that help you be ready for one of life's most beautiful gifts. Placing your heart in God's hands will help guide you the rest of the way. "I have stilled my soul, like a weaned child to its mother, weaned is my soul," says the writer of Psalm 131.

 How have you put your trust in God's hands in the past? How are you putting your heart and soul in God's hands in preparation for your baby? Does your image of God take on a feminine image like that of the psalmist?

_____

_____

_____

_____

_____

_____

_____

_____

_____

Feeling Gorgeous

She chose sandals for her feet, and put on her anklets, bracelets, rings, earrings, and all her other jewelry. Thus she made herself very beautiful, to entice the eyes of all the men who would see her.

JUDITH 10:4

You might not feel like a million bucks these days, especially if morning sickness has hit you hard. Maybe there are certain smells or food you just can't stand. Your body is starting to feel alien to you or maybe it just needs time to adjust to your new normal.

Everything that is happening now with food, smells, and hormones will most likely fade in the second trimester. Although your due date seems far off, it will come up fast. Physically you may feel ill, yet inside there is a beauty as your baby is growing. The tiny human is getting ready to meet you and every week is a step closer to the outside world.

Some days you may not feel beautiful, but you are very beautiful despite the mood swings, cravings, and perhaps nausea. As you begin your third month of pregnancy, think about what makes you feel beautiful. Think about how your beauty shows despite morning sickness or discomfort. In the Book of

Judith we see a woman readying herself. "She chose sandals for her feet, and put on her anklets, bracelets, rings, earrings, and all her other jewelry. Thus she made herself very beautiful, to entice the eyes of all the men who would see her."

Today, ask yourself what makes you feel beautiful. Is it something you wore? Or maybe just an inner confidence you rocked that made you feel beautiful? List a few ways that you can nurture yourself in these weeks of pregnancy that will help you feel confident and beautiful in your journey.

_____

_____

_____

_____

_____

First Photos

*For I know well the
plans I have in mind
for you—oracle of the
Lord—plans for your
welfare and not for woe,
so as to give you
a future of hope.*

JEREMIAH 29:11

This week may be the ultrasound week, or it might be right around the corner for you. It's exciting to see the image and even more special to see the response in your spouse's eyes.

The life you created is no doubt beautiful in every way. You know how breathtaking it was to learn you were pregnant, and now to see it in front of you makes it more real. The tiny head and body are just a couple of centimeters long, but the way in which your heart has grown these past months brings gratitude.

Your baby's first ultrasound may be a secret you and your husband share between you, or it might make its way around to family and friends. No matter how you share or savor this first picture of your baby, cherish these moments of laying eyes on your beloved. Your pregnancy will continue to unfold for you in coming months. It may be a

smooth path or one with a few obstacles. Through it all, know and feel God's presence and plan for your life. Know and trust in God's plan for you. Remember God's words in the Book of Jeremiah: "For I know well the plans I have in mind for you—oracle of the Lord—plans for your welfare and not for woe, so as to give you a future of hope."

 If you have seen your first ultrasound picture, what were your initial words and thoughts? Is there anything about having the ultrasound in your possession that makes the pregnancy more real for you and your husband?

_____

_____

_____

_____

_____

Power and Love

For this reason, I remind you to stir into flame the gift of God that you have through the imposition of my hands. For God did not give us the spirit of cowardice but rather of power and love and self control.

2 Timothy 1:6–7

Being toward the end of the first trimester means you have made it through the first part of pregnancy. Maybe some of your fears have disappeared, especially if you worried about having a miscarriage early on. Maybe some of your fears are still on the horizon. There is much to learn on this new road.

It's a big leap moving from married couple to family of three. There is probably so much going on in your life these days that bringing your baby into the world may bring you fear and anxiety. Or maybe you have health-related concerns that you will have to face before your baby is born. It's hard to let go of control and know God is holding you, guiding you and alongside you all at the same time.

Maybe preparing for the baby's birth can help you lean more into God's trust. We see in the Second Letter to Timothy the importance of leaning on God's

Spirit: "For this reason, I remind you to stir into flame the gift of God that you have through the imposition of my hands. For God did not give us the spirit of cowardice but rather of power and love and self control."

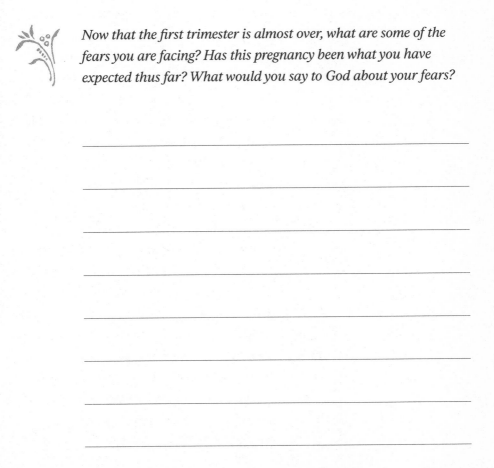

Now that the first trimester is almost over, what are some of the fears you are facing? Has this pregnancy been what you have expected thus far? What would you say to God about your fears?

Making the Sacrifice

And to offer the sacrifice of "a pair of turtledoves or two young pigeons," in accordance with the dictate in the law of the Lord.

LUKE 2:24

Learning to ease into motherhood isn't something that happens overnight. Your body transforms slowly alongside your heart. Your habits transform. You move from selfish to selfless. The physical changes in your body are preparing you carry the child for many more months. You are the sole and soul provider of your child. Your body is no longer just *your* body as it nurtures and protects another being. You move toward sacrificing things you might like to eat during pregnancy to things that are better for baby.

Every week is a new opportunity to make small and large sacrifices. The transformation from current-you to the mother God has called you to be is real. Today those sacrifices could be giving up a den or office for your baby's bedroom or saving extra money to help cover the new costs. Maybe it means less extravagant vacations and individual purchases. In the Gospel of

Luke we see the sacrifice Mary and Joseph made in the temple. "And to offer the sacrifice of 'a pair of turtledoves or two young pigeons,' in accordance with the dictate in the law of the Lord."

What are some sacrifices you have made for your baby thus far? What do you imagine you and your husband will give up in the next year for the baby? What sacrifices do you feel God is asking you to make?

_____

_____

_____

_____

_____

_____

A Time for Everything

There is an appointed time for everything, and a time for every affair under the heavens. A time to give birth, and a time to die; a time to plant, and a time to uproot the plant.

ECCLESIASTES 3:1–2

T ime is of the essence these days. It seems to slip through your fingers as you prepare for baby's arrival. There are things you are deciding on the fly. There is extra rest you are taking. Time is like sand running through your fingers.

The postpartum period feels far away, yet you have probably inquired about your workplace's policy on maternity leave. Maybe you can only take six weeks or, if you are lucky, a few months. Some women dip into savings to make it work. It's important to take time away from work responsibilities to bond with your baby. You will also need healing time for your body.

Breathe through this planning period. In some ways time takes on a more sacred meaning as your family is growing. We see an informed passage about time in the book of Ecclesiastes that may help shape our sense of preparation. "There is an appointed

time for everything, and a time for every affair under the heavens: A time to give birth, and a time to die; a time to plant, and a time to uproot the plant."

How much time do you want to take with your baby after the birth? If you are currently working, do you think you will return to work? Are you finding any disappointment in how little support companies provide to new mothers and fathers? What would you say to God about asking for help in finding time to prepare for motherhood?

_____

_____

_____

_____

_____

_____

Giving Thanks

Then Hannah spoke up: "Excuse me, my lord! As you live, my lord, I am the woman who stood here near you, praying to the LORD. I prayed for this child, and the LORD granted my request."

1 SAMUEL 1:26–27

Your news of the pregnancy may have spread around your different communities by now. You hear words of congratulations and answered prayers. Your own prayer might be one of thanksgiving and anxiety at the same time. That baby growing inside of you may bring about mixed emotions, and that's a very real truth about pregnancy.

Maybe this baby is a complete surprise or one you had planned to conceive. There are always opportunities to be thankful and generous with this gift God has shared with you and your husband. There is also an honesty in knowing this baby may bring about some anxiety. It's a mixed bag coming into motherhood, and it's your bag to hold for today and always.

The thankful emotions you have might not match a Hallmark card or a Lifetime movie, but they are your real words of gratitude. It's also possible to be fuzzy and gray some days as you

adapt to your new body and new reality. It's never too much to thank God over and over. In the First Book of Samuel, we see Hannah sharing her thanksgiving for her child: "Excuse me, my lord! As you live, my lord, I am the woman who stood here near you, praying to the LORD. I prayed for this child, and the LORD granted my request."

 How have you shared your gratitude with God for your baby? Can you name exactly what you are thankful for? Is there some anxiety mixed in with thanksgiving? How are you sharing that with God?

_____

_____

_____

_____

_____

_____

Mary and Martha

[Martha] had a sister named Mary [who] sat beside the Lord at his feet listening to him speak. Martha, burdened with much serving, came to him and said, "Lord, do you not care that my sister has left me by myself to do the serving? Tell her to help me." The Lord said to her in reply, "Martha, Martha, you are anxious and worried about many things. There is need of only one thing. Mary has chosen the better part and it will not be taken from her."

LUKE 10:39–42

You might be feeling like the Energizer Bunny these days. Maybe you feel like your old self in some ways. Your energy might be closer to pre-pregnancy, as morning sickness is most likely a thing of the past. Maybe your energy is coming from the excitement of having a baby or you go into overdrive with planning everything.

Your extra energy may be going into preparations at home. Or maybe you are checking out maternity clothes sales or enjoying one-on-one time with friends and family. Amid this flurry of activity, you may catch yourself smiling more often. Or perhaps you are a list creator, tracking things that need to be done in coming months. Or perhaps you are taking more downtime for yourself. This time of energy and preparation is reminiscent of Martha and Mary in the Gospel of Luke: "[Martha] had a sister named Mary [who] sat beside the Lord at his feet listening to him speak. Martha,

burdened with much serving, came to him and said, 'Lord, do you not care that my sister has left me by myself to do the serving? Tell her to help me.' The Lord said to her in reply, 'Martha, Martha, you are anxious and worried about many things. There is need of only one thing. Mary has chosen the better part and it will not be taken from her.'"

Given the short description of these two women—which do you more closely relate to right now? Are you keeping busy in preparation? Are you making time to spend time with the Lord? If so, what does that look like for you?

Boy or Girl?

Then God said: Let us make human beings in our image, after our likeness. Let them have dominion over the fish of the sea, the birds of the air, the tame animals, all the wild animals, and all the creatures that crawl on the earth.

GENESIS 1:26

s you approach twenty weeks, people will ask you, "Do you know if it's a boy or a girl?" Maybe you have decided to find out your baby's gender, or maybe you are waiting until the day you deliver. Or maybe you and are your husband are split on this, and one of you will find out this week and the other in the delivery room.

Whatever choice you and your husband make is the right choice. It's really exciting either way. If you find out now, there is more planning that can go into your pregnancy with clothes and perhaps your baby's room décor. And if it's a surprise, there is anticipation that fills your days and weeks that's just a tad bit different.

Either way you decide, there's a good chance you have a sense of names, even if it's just a list of favorite boy's and girl's names. You might be thinking of naming your child after a friend or family member. Or maybe it's a name

you or your husband have always loved. Savor these moments of anticipation and wonder, knowing that God has already created your son or daughter in God's image, as we hear in the Book of Genesis: "Let us make human beings in our image, after our likeness. Let them have dominion over the fish of the sea, the birds of the air, the tame animals, all the wild animals, and all the creatures that crawl on the earth."

Have you and your husband decided to find out your baby's gender? Will you keep it to yourselves or share with the world? Do you spend time imagining what features your baby will share you with and your husband?

Facing My Fears

The beginning of wisdom is to fear the Lord; she is created with the faithful in the womb. With the godly she was created from of old, and with their descendants she will keep the faith.

SIRACH 1:14–15

These weeks in the second trimester are creeping closer to your halfway point. Soon you will be counting down the weeks until you meet your beloved. Imagine for a moment the spaces in your body that are longing to meet your child. Your heart will have a new person to love— and that person will be in your arms. Your eyes are longing to gaze on your baby's face. And your fingers will have a little one to caress.

Active waiting to meet your child is a beautiful time of life. There is no other active waiting time like this. Maybe your first trimester was difficult with morning sickness, or maybe it was a breeze. The second trimester is typically the one in which most women feel the best.

Each day that passes gives you more opportunities to hone your decision-making skills for you and baby. In the Book of Sirach, we see a reference to motherhood and wisdom. "The

beginning of wisdom is to fear the Lord; she is created with the faithful in the womb. With the godly she was created from of old, and with their descendants she will keep the faith."

How are you feeling about being near the halfway point to meeting your child? What are you hoping to pass on to your child? What real fears do you have about childbirth? What real fears do you have about parenthood?

_____

_____

_____

_____

_____

_____

Time Together

"Now, not with lust, but with fidelity I take this kinswoman as my wife. Send down your mercy on me and on her and grant that we may grow old together. Bless us with children."

TOBIT 8:7

These tender days before your twosome grows to three are numbered. Impromptu date nights and long and lazy outings will be a thing of the past once baby arrives. Whether you have been married one year or several years, spending time with your husband is always a time to be cherished.

The phrase "never stop dating your spouse" is true. If you stop and think about your relationship, you know that one exact moment you fell for your beloved. It was one memory burned into your mind that told you he was the one to spend all your days with forever. He was the one you knew your heart wanted as a forever partner to build your family. This season of life is for building.

It's amazing and scary, but your husband was put into your life to be part of this moment. You are each other's treasure. In the Book of Tobit we see

Tobiah and Sarah praying and asking for an opportunity to grow old together and have children. "Now," says Tobiah, "not with lust, but with fidelity I take this kinswoman as my wife. Send down your mercy on me and on her, and grant that we may grow old together. Bless us with children."

What is your favorite memory of a date with your husband? What about that date makes it special for you? What is one quality you admire about your husband that you hope your child inherits?

_____

_____

_____

_____

_____

_____

Learning to Move

"For at the moment the sound of your greeting reached my ears, the infant in my womb leaped for joy."

LUKE 1:44

Movement along your belly may feel like gas or maybe a little bit ticklish depending on your baby's activity. It's uncomfortable and beautiful at the same time. And it's hard to believe this little one belongs to you. There's a good chance you have been feeling flutter kicks this week or maybe even earlier. Maybe you smiled or shed happy tears the first time you felt your baby kick. Or if you were with your husband you grabbed his hand and put it on your belly—because this moment is one to cherish for both of you.

It's an unmistakable feeling of grace to connect with your child in this way. You might not even be feeling these moments on a frequent basis, but they take your breath away when they happen. There's nothing more beautiful, right? This feeling of surprise and delight does not get old. The movement may feel uncomfortable in the last

weeks, but today and right now it's a way for your baby to share life with you. Feeling your baby move around is similar to the moment that Elizabeth felt her infant leap in her womb as Mary approached: "For at the moment the sound of your greeting reached my ears, the infant in my womb leaped for joy."

Where were you when you first felt the baby move?
How does it feel knowing the infant is growing inside you?
Did the sensation feel like you expected it to feel when the baby first kicked or moved?

_____

_____

_____

_____

_____

_____

Precious in God's Eyes

*Because you
are precious in my
eyes and honored,
and I love you.*

ISAIAH 43:4

This is sometimes a big week in pregnancy because of what you see in your baby's ultrasound: gender, potential abnormalities, and even issues with growth. It's exciting to again see your baby growing before your eyes. You'll look at their tiny legs and feet. You will see their fingers and hands. You will see their heart beating. It's just so real now.

During this ultrasound you may also discover a potential abnormality or other health-related issue that you have to face. Prepare your heart for all that will be revealed this time around. You and your husband have made many plans both outwardly with each other and maybe quietly in your own hearts. Laying your eyes on your baby can be a reminder of your love for each other. In the Book of Isaiah we can see how precious we are in God's eyes. Your baby is already cherished in your eyes and will continue to be as you progress

onward. "Because you are precious in my eyes and honored," God says, "and I love you." God says.

As you prepare for or reflect on your latest ultrasound, what has changed since you first saw your baby on screen? What about your son or daughter already makes them precious in your eyes? What fears do you have this week, if you and the doctors discovered something that may not be normal?

_____

_____

_____

_____

_____

_____

Feeding Body, Mind, and Spirit

Go, eat your bread with joy and drink your wine with a merry heart, because it is now that God favors your works.

ECCLESIASTES 9:7

That voracious appetite of yours may be your excuse to snack or munch your way through the week. Now that morning sickness is behind you, you may be back to enjoying your favorite foods or perhaps enjoying new ones your body is eagerly craving.

Friends, family, and even strangers will sometimes share their food stories with you. They'll share their cravings or aversions. As your bump grows, you are slowly learning to accept your new body for all of its beauty and newfound curves. Eating with people and celebrating with them, especially in this time of joyful anticipation, will be part of your experience. There is something irresistibly communal about food. In Ecclesiastes we see food and celebration going hand in hand: "Go, eat your bread with joy and drink your wine with a merry heart, because it is now that God favors your works."

 What are some of your favorite cravings right now? What are some food items that you just don't have a taste for? How are you continuing to celebrate your pregnancy with family and friends? What are some ways to feed your soul that don't include food or drink?

_____

_____

_____

_____

_____

_____

_____

_____

_____

Sacred Moments

I too am mortal, the same as all the rest, and a descendant of the first one formed of earth. And in my mother's womb I was molded into flesh...

WISDOM 7:1

Stolen and sacred moments with your bump are part of your everyday life now. Maybe you and your bump enjoy quiet mornings while you have a cup of tea or decaf coffee. Or maybe it's a walk through the halls at work or when you share a tidbit about your day or share a whisper with your beloved. However these stolen and sacred moments come to you, embrace them as your life.

Knowing you are growing a child is absolutely beautiful. It's probably unmistakable now that you are carrying a human. In some ways it's like sharing some big and small secrets together. Marvel in God's goodness in you bringing life into this world. Not all days of pregnancy are bliss and smooth sailing. Some days are challenging, and maybe you do receive disappointing news about your baby's growth. It's a balance every step of the way. In the Book of Wisdom we hear about

a mother's womb and the growth that accompanies a baby: "I too am mortal, the same as all the rest, and a descendant of the first one formed of earth. And in my mother's womb I was molded into flesh..."

As moments of quiet become part of your daily rhythms, what do you tell your baby when it's just the two of you? Do you have a favorite time or place to have those conversations? Does your husband also share quiet time with the baby? What does he say to your beloved?

_____

_____

_____

_____

_____

_____

Our Blessed Mother

"The Mighty One has done great things for me, and holy is his name."

LUKE 1:49

Finding mom mentors in pregnancy is as important as other aspects of baby preparations. Sharing your journey with other moms or even moms-to-be is a great way to prepare your heart for what's next in your life. There's a shift into an unknown that will come along with motherhood. Your identity and brain cells are going to be constantly adjusting to continue your transition to your new life.

Mom or mother is more than a title. It's truly a vocation that you are also sharing with Mary, our Blessed Mother. Her pregnancy aches and joys may match yours. Maybe you already have a strong devotion to her and have no qualms about calling out to "Mama Mary" in your life. Or maybe she's someone you want to get to know better as part of your prayer journey in pregnancy.

Her living example of pregnancy and uncertainty gives way to trust in

God. She is a beacon to follow when we feel stuck or even need some inspiration. She proclaims God's greatness as part of the Magnificat and recognizes her humility. "The Mighty One has done great things for me," she says, "and holy is his name."

Who are the moms in your life, either living or deceased, that you admire? What traits do you admire in them? How comfortable are you praying to Mary as part of your pregnancy? What do you share with her?

_____

_____

_____

_____

_____

_____

Staying Healthy

Beloved, I hope you are prospering in every respect and are in good health, just as your soul is prospering.

3 JOHN 1:2

Minor aches and bloating are just part of the game these days. There is slight discomfort when you are awake, and slight discomfort when you sleep. It's pretty easy to come home after work and just sleep because you are exhausted. Growing and carrying a child is difficult work.

Merely considering exercise in the first trimester may have seemed impossible, depending how morning sickness treated you. At this point you have about three months left, so carrying your baby isn't going to get easier. You'll feel heavier each week with no relief in sight.

Maybe you really enjoy exercise, so you are flying through pregnancy figuring out your own routine. Or perhaps exercise has never been a part of your adult life. Exercise does keep you and your baby healthy, even if it's a walk after work or during your lunch

hour, if you can manage it. Health and fitness in pregnancy can be fun once you find the right fit for your body and for this pregnancy. In the Third Letter of John we hear about health and wellness: "Beloved, I hope you are prospering in every respect and are in good health, just as your soul is prospering."

What are your favorite exercises in pregnancy? If you don't have one yet, what is stopping you from exercising? Are there health-related issues you are facing that are causing extra stress?

_____

_____

_____

_____

_____

Feathering the Nest

Collecting baby items, either in your future nursery or in your online shopping carts, may be taking up some of your time as you prepare for baby's arrival. There are so many decisions to make between car seats, cribs, and carriers that your head will spin. You might be checking YouTube reviews or mommy blogs for the most up-to-date information. You most likely have begun assembling your baby registry or bookmarking pages in your Internet browser for baby furniture.

This is definitely a time for list-making and knowledge collecting. Some couples choose to have an extensive baby wish list and others keep it simple and see what they need once baby arrives. It's easy to jump down the rabbit hole and get lost in Facebook groups or Pinterest pages. Enjoy this time of preparation and collection. This beautiful anticipation of your baby is contagious with family and friends.

In the Letter to the Hebrews we see the importance of living a life free from money and too many things: "Let your life be free from love of money but be content with what you have, for he has said, 'I will never forsake you or abandon you.'"

What are some of your necessary items for baby? What does it mean for you to help provide for your growing family? Is this time fun or stressful? Why is that?

_____

_____

_____

_____

_____

_____

Preparing for Parenthood

*"Let the children
come to me, and
do not prevent them;
for the kingdom
of heaven belongs to
such as these..."*

Matthew 19:14

ssembling the nursery and picking out items for your registry might seem like a breeze compared to your first parenting class. Some parents wait until the last month of pregnancy and others tackle classes early in the second trimester. Depending on where you live, there may be many options for parenting and birthing classes; it is tough to know where to begin and what's necessary for you and your husband.

Preparing for your baby will probably feel more real when you do show up to your first class, especially if the class includes baby mannequins on the table when you first walk in. There are choices among choices in deciding what classes you want or need. You may even take a class solo for breastfeeding or sleep training. Whatever the case is for you, take the time to learn in a way that pushes you to grow as a parent.

No matter what class or classes you

take, know that God planted a seed deep in your heart asking you to take on the vocation of motherhood long before you even knew it was in your future. This sacred and sometimes fleeting time is your time to prepare. "Let the children come to me, and do not prevent them," Jesus says; "for the kingdom of heaven belongs to such as these."

 What classes are you enrolled in or hoping to enroll in before the baby is born? What books are you reading to help you prepare? Why did you choose these books or these classes? Does learning about your baby excite you? Why?

_____

_____

_____

_____

_____

_____

Praying for Healing

*Heal me, Lord,
that I may be healed;
save me, that I may
be saved, for you
are my praise.*

JEREMIAH 17:14

Even the healthiest of diets and being in the best physical health are no guarantee that a baby or mother is safe against complications. It's hard not to get emotional if you learn that you or your baby has a health issue that you will have to face in the third trimester. Perhaps when you made it past twelve weeks, you were thinking that everything was ok. And when you hit twenty weeks and did another scan, you may have continued to coast.

Working with physicians and nurses in preparation for your baby's safe arrival could mean other plans for you and your baby that you had not considered. No one is eager to tackle complications, but sometimes your journey to motherhood may include more challenges than you bargained for. Keep close to your heart the prayer of the prophet Jeremiah: "Heal me, Lord, that I may be healed; save me, that I may be saved, for you are my praise."

What would you ask healing for this week, and why are you asking for it? How is your health and the baby's health?
If everything seems OK right now, what fears do you have for the last months of the pregnancy?

_____

_____

_____

_____

_____

_____

_____

_____

_____

Finding Peace

"Peace I leave you;
my peace I give you.
Not as the world gives
do I give it to you.
Do not let your hearts
be troubled or afraid."

JOHN 14:27

Sleepless nights are probably starting to add up this week. If it isn't discomfort from your back and side, maybe it's the thoughts racing in your mind. You may be asking yourself if everything will be ready. You may be spending time on Google or asking friends about how you'll know when you're ready to have your baby. Some people will tell you that you will know when the baby is placed in your arms.

It's easy to get caught up in the anxiety of the unknown and all the "what if" questions you are asking yourself all night long as you toss and turn. It's easy to tell someone to turn off their brain and just rest. Try not to get carried away by all that is to come. Trust that God will continue to lead you through these days and weeks. "Peace I leave you; my peace I give you," Jesus says. "Not as the world gives do I give it to you. Do not let your hearts be troubled or afraid."

What kind of peace are you seeking today? How many hours a night are you sleeping this week? And how can you try and get more rest for you and your baby? What's one thing you can try this week or next week to give your mind a rest?

_____

_____

_____

_____

_____

_____

_____

_____

Asking for Help

"Ask and it will be given to you; seek and you will find; knock and the door will be opened to you."

MATTHEW 7:7

Restrictions on lifting and exercise may have hampered your plans in recent weeks. It's harder to pick things up, and everyone at work may be offering to give you a hand to do just about everything. People in stores may be offering to open doors and help as well. Strangers pick up things you have dropped. You may find yourself asking for help constantly. Maybe before you were pregnant you struggled asking others for help even if they are close to you.

Next time you think you can't ask for help from a stranger or coworker, take a breath and count to five before voicing your request. People truly want to help; it's just a matter of letting them know how to assist. "Ask and it will be given to you," Jesus said; "seek and you will find; knock and the door will be opened to you."

 How have you asked for help today? This week? What is one thing you used to be able to do that you can't do during this stage of the pregnancy? If it's hard to ask for help, why is that?

_____

_____

_____

_____

_____

_____

_____

_____

Aches and Pains

We know that all creation is groaning in labor pains even until now.

ROMANS 8:22

ching ankles and a heavy belly...the simplest walk can leave you breathless. Maybe there's a slight feeling of arthritis in your fingers and joints. You are sore and maybe feel just plain heavy. You ask yourself what normal even feels like these days as you adjust the elastic band around your belly to help take the pressure off your lower back.

You are out of relaxing positions; sitting and standing are uncomfortable. Pillows definitely give comfort and support at the end of a long day. It's no fun, but you are getting closer to delivery day: you are about to get into single digits as you count down the weeks until you meet your baby. All of these pains in pregnancy may give you a story to tell when you meet your baby. You understand in a new way what St. Paul meant in his Letter to the Romans when he said: "We know that all creation is groaning in labor pains even until now."

What aches right now? How long have you been uncomfortable in your body? What about this experience makes you thankful for your journey to start a family?

_____

_____

_____

_____

_____

_____

_____

_____

_____

"Momnesia"

Can a mother forget her infant, be without tenderness for the child of her womb? Even should she forget, I will never forget you.

ISAIAH 49:15

Have you been forgetting your keys, wallet, or personal appointments because of what has been called "pregnancy brain"? Maybe reminder notes or alarms on your phone are now your new normal!

Having a hard time remembering everything that's asked of you is sometimes referred to as "momnesia." You are trying to remember if you took your prenatal vitamins, rescheduled an appointment with your doctor, or maybe even tried to fit in time with a good friend. And on top of forgetting things, sleepless nights and exhaustion are making your brain work overtime. Maybe you laugh off your memory lapses as another temporary casualty of pregnancy, or perhaps it becomes a real excuse for why you are just all over the place these days.

Today's forgetfulness will end, and soon your brain will be back to its old self, except for the accommodations it

makes for baby. You may forget errands and appointments, but you will never forget the experience and gift of carrying your child. In the Book of Isaiah, we hear how God never forgets us, comparing it to a mom never forgetting her child: "Can a mother forget her infant, be without tenderness for the child of her womb? Even should she forget, I will never forget you."

What are some major things you have forgotten in the past few months? How did it make you feel to realize you were forgetting a few things you normally would have remembered? How do you hope to remember this pregnancy?

_____

_____

_____

_____

_____

Finding the Rhythm

Addressing one another in psalms, hymns and spiritual songs, singing and playing to the Lord in your hearts.

EPHESIANS 5:19

By now, your baby recognizes your voice. It's a sweet sound to your little one. You and your husband may already be talking and singing to your baby on a regular basis. Or maybe you giggle together, talking about all the possibilities for the three of you. Some parents will listen to classical music with their baby bump, and others continue rocking out to pop songs.

Music is a wonderful way for you to bond with the baby in your womb. There may even be old favorites you and your husband enjoy singing to your baby every night as part of an evening routine. It's like magic, connecting to your baby in a way that can make your own heart sing. Music might be an important part of your life if you enjoy singing or playing a musical instrument. Music and song may also be the way you connect to God in a special way, whether it's personal in your car or

public at a praise and worship night. In the Letter to the Ephesians we see how psalms and songs connect us to God: "addressing one another in psalms, hymns and spiritual songs, singing and playing to the Lord in your hearts."

Which songs have you chosen to sing to your baby in the womb?
What are some of your favorite nursery rhymes from childhood?
What are some things you want to share with your baby these days?

_____

_____

_____

_____

_____

_____

Becoming a Family

"And I have given them the glory you gave me, so that they may be one, as we are one."

JOHN 17:22

Your forever twosome is about to add a forever teammate. It's a fun time, a time of joy; but let's face it: you know the evolution of "us" is now about to shift. You absolutely love your husband, and you love the time you spend time together. It's getting real now as the bump sticks out a little more each week.

The stolen glances that make you smile will soon make way for late-night diapers and "honey, can you grab this or that." All of that shifting is good, but the wistful get-up-and-go of your relationship will be put on hold for a while as you raise your child. In these remaining days as a family of two, allow yourselves to celebrate the uniqueness of your marriage. Even if this child is the answer to months or years of prayers, there may be some sadness in saying goodbye to you as a couple.

But even with children, you and your husband are united forever. When you

stood before each other on your wedding day, the two of you—without losing your individuality and different personalities—were becoming one, a singular unit recognized in God's eyes. In the Gospel of John, we see the importance of two becoming one. Jesus says, "And I have given them the glory you gave me, so that they may be one, as we are one."

What are your favorite parts about what it means to be "us"?
Where have you grown as a couple since your wedding day?
What are you afraid of losing when your baby arrives?

_____

_____

_____

_____

_____

_____

Growing in Love

Love is patient, love is kind. It is not jealous, love is not pompous, it is not inflated, it is not rude, it does not seek its own interests, it is not quick-tempered, it does not brood over injury, it does not rejoice over wrongdoing but rejoices with the truth.

1 CORINTHIANS 13:4

D-day—as in delivery day—is fast approaching, and you will be using your new-parent skills in no time. Your ever-changing body continues to prepare you and your baby for her or his entrance into the world. Your baby may have settled into a head-down position or might still need a week or two to turn over. It's a matter of time now as you wait patiently, or maybe impatiently. If you are a planner, perhaps you have read all the symptoms and signs of early labor just in case it happens—like *now*. Or maybe you have a more go-with- the-flow attitude, and you know the baby will pop out when he or she is ready to meet the world.

This time of waiting actively is coming closer to the moment of surrendering yourself to a tiny human. Your body is supporting another life, so what you eat and drink isn't just for you. You realize you need more rest

for the both of you. These physical changes show a need to surrender, for your body is no longer yours. In his Letter to the Corinthians, St. Paul describes the kind of love that emerges as you become a parent: "Love is patient, love is kind. It is not jealous, love is not pompous, it is not inflated, it is not rude, it does not seek its own interests, it is not quick-tempered, it does not brood over injury, it does not rejoice over wrongdoing but rejoices with the truth."

What are some of the ways you have already surrendered to your baby? How has your heart grown in love? How are you passing the time until your baby arrives?

_____

_____

_____

_____

_____

_____

Facing the Pain

As a woman is about to give birth writhes and cries out in pain, so were we before you, Lord.

ISAIAH 26:17

By now you have most likely completed some parent classes and done a fair share of reading about vaginal births and cesarean sections. Maybe you've entered the word "epidural" into Google search a few times to read medical articles and mommy blogs about it. Perhaps you have also joined Facebook groups to help prepare you for the pain of labor and the long recovery after your child is born. Your brain is wired and prepared to handle the pain.

Moms in your life let you know how it's all worth it to see your little peanut in your arms. The unknown of when baby is arriving, coupled with what the actual pain of labor will feel like, can make you a little uneasy, especially if you like to know a lot in advance. You have seen the movies and maybe have dreamt about how your day will play out if you are having a vaginal delivery. For other moms who are having a C-section the

anxiety may be thinking about how your body will heal post-delivery.

Whether it's not knowing what the pain will feel like or just being a little anxious about how and when baby decides to enter the world, there is plenty to fear. Isaiah shares with us what the pain of labor can look like before the beauty of your child is before your eyes: "As a woman is about to give birth writhes and cries out in pain, so were we before you, Lord."

What gives you the most anxiety about your baby's birth? How have you prepared yourself emotionally? Physically? What's the best piece of advice you have received for your delivery?

_____

_____

_____

_____

_____

_____

Final Preparations

She girds herself with strength; she exerts her arms with vigor. She enjoys the profits from her dealings; her lamp is never extinguished at night.

PROVERBS 31:17–18

*N*ewborn onesies and your outfit for bringing baby home have already been washed and set aside. Maybe you picked a personalized outfit with your child's name printed on it. Or perhaps you are not sure if you're having a boy or a girl, so you have one of each outfit set aside for the day they come home. You and your husband have been busily preparing your hearts and your home for this next chapter of your lives.

By now, some relatives and friends have probably come over to help you prepare the baby's space. Perhaps they assembled baby furniture or helped you install the infant car seat. Mountains of clothes have been washed, dried, and put away until your son or daughter arrives. You may be simultaneously preparing coworkers and your employer for maternity leave. The work may seem nonstop for you, and it may be getting later in the evening before you can finally quiet your mind to get ready for

bed. As the Book of Proverbs says of the Woman of Worth, "She girds herself with strength; she exerts her arms with vigor. She enjoys the profits from her dealings; her lamp is never extinguished at night." Still, it's important to remember that getting rest is just as important as all your other preparations.

In this homestretch, how are you making final preparations for your baby's arrival? Who has been helping, and how have they contributed? What are some things you think you can leave until after baby is born? Or even get a relative or friend to take over for you?

_____

_____

_____

_____

_____

What Are You Bringing with You?

> *"Do not take gold or silver or copper for your belts; no sack for the journey, or a second tunic, or sandals or a walking stick."*
>
> **MATTHEW 10:9–10**

s you are preparing yourself for your hospital stay, you have many options for what to include in your bag. Lists are available from the internet and social media on what is most essential for labor and a short hospital stay. Some moms may use nothing they pack in their bag, and others need most of things in their bag to stay comfortable. You may want a tablet for movies and music, and a phone charger. Pack comfortable clothes, such as a robe and comfy and cute pajamas to wear when people come to visit and, of course, for super adorable photos with your newborn. And depending on how long you will be laboring, snacks are always key to keeping your energy up.

Whatever is thrown into your bag for that exact moment you head out the door to the hospital is the right thing to include. You may find yourself using many of the hospital's items for

the duration of your stay. It's hard to know what will be helpful until you are there. This journey of parenthood includes everything *and* the kitchen sink these days! But be prudent about what you will really need. In the Gospel of Matthew, we see how Jesus told his disciples to prepare for their next journey of mission; they were to take nothing and to trust in him: "Do not take gold or silver or copper for your belts; no sack for the journey, or a second tunic, or sandals or a walking stick."

What are some items you have packed in your bag that will help you be comfortable? What are some items you have packed for baby?

_____

_____

_____

_____

_____

Waiting and Wondering

A voice proclaims:
In the wilderness
prepare the way of the
Lord! Make straight
in the wasteland a
highway for our God.

ISAIAH 40:3

You may experience bouts of nesting and preparing—as well as exhaustion— in this third trimester. It's a time of patience and maybe disbelief that your baby is almost here. Only a short time now before you meet your beloved. Aside from readying yourself and baby for your hospital stay, there are preparations at home. Maybe you or a relative are stocking your freezer with stews or soups. Then there is late-night cleaning to help you ready your space for your baby and any relatives who might be coming into town to help after the birth.

You feel mostly ready, but maybe there are things you feel you're forgetting. The parenting and birth classes have been taken. You discussed your maternity leave with your supervisor and are ready if baby comes in two weeks or even today. You have even thought about your post-baby photo shoot outfit for you and baby.

The only one missing is your child, and you are ready to see their face and squeeze them tight. You and your husband are probably as ready as you are going to be for your baby. Take comfort in knowing the best part is just around the bend. As Isaiah wrote, "A voice proclaims: In the wilderness prepare the way of the Lord! Make straight in the wasteland a highway for our God."

 How does it feel to be days from meeting your baby? Do you feel ready? If not, what would you like to do in the next week or two? What is still on your to-do list?

_____

_____

_____

_____

_____

_____

Praying for a Safe Delivery

*Yes, I hear the cry,
like that of a woman in
labor, like the anguish
of a mother bearing
her first child.*

JEREMIAH 4:31

By now, you have established your birth plan with your obstetrician, and you are praying all goes well. Maybe you have asked friends and relatives about the birth stories of their children. You hear how quick or slow labor seemed for some women. Others advise you not to ask those questions this late in the game because your anxiety may creep higher than you wish. When you attended the birth class with your husband you learned there were clear differences in labor. And most advised you to labor at home as long as possible, because it's hard to know how long it will take once you are at the hospital.

And if you are having a C-section the process isn't as prolonged, but because it's major surgery, it may definitely produce some anxiety. Whatever way your child will be ushered into the world is a special and unique experience for you and your husband. This baby is the

baby that officially makes you parents. As the big day approaches, keep in mind how much stress your body will endure, from the active labor to recovery process. You may not seem all that fragile but know that your body is fragile as you are carrying another life inside you. Take whatever steps you can to rest, because your baby will be here before you know it. "Yes," says the prophet Jeremiah, "I hear the cry, like that of a woman in labor, like the anguish of a mother bearing her first child."

Who is going to be with you in the delivery room? Why did you select them to join you? How are you going to capture the moment you first meet your child?

_____

_____

_____

_____

_____

Welcoming a New Life

*She gave birth
to her firstborn son,
She wrapped him in
swaddling clothes and
laid him in a manger,
because there was
no room for them
at the inn.*

LUKE 2:6–7

Chances are if this is your first child you may still have a few more days to go before you meet your baby. Some people around you may share with you how late their first baby was. It's been nothing but preparation for you these past few weeks. Maybe you've attempted to nap every chance you've had, and tried to sleep in even more the last few weekends, because as everyone has remarked, you may not sleep much in the first months or even first year.

Now the fun begins as you wait and count down the minutes and seconds. There may be chaos in your delivery and labor journey, or perhaps it will all appear calm. Maybe you have been experiencing Braxton Hicks contractions the past few weeks and are just waiting for the real ones to begin. As you and your husband continue to count down the minutes to meeting your little one, talk to your baby, who probably can't wait to meet you as well.

Think of the birth of Jesus: "She gave birth to her firstborn son. She wrapped him in swaddling clothes and laid him in a manger, because there was no room for them at the inn."

Do you imagine your baby's birth will be chaos or calm? What are some things you may ask Mary for this week as you prepare for your delivery? What if anything do you think you will miss about your pregnancy?

Prayer to the Holy Family

(INSPIRED BY *AMORIS LAETITIA*)

Jesus, Mary, and Joseph, we give thanks to you today and always
for our family; we ask you to watch over us always.

Holy Family of Nazareth, grant that our family may be a place
of love, and our home be a place of peace.

Holy Family of Nazareth, as we navigate these early days as a family,
guide us in patience, and help us find rest.

Holy Family of Nazareth, help us to remember to turn to you often
for guidance. Remind us always that our family is holy like you.

Graciously hear our prayer. Amen.

BABY'S NAME

BABY'S DATE OF BIRTH

BABY'S WEIGHT AND LENGTH

LOCATION OF DELIVERY